Becoming Me: Reflection and Insight Through Poetry and Prose

A. L. Hearn

DEDICATION

I dedicate this book back to God Himself as a first fruits from the spoils derived from the tests of faith through which courage, resilience, creativity, and an even greater level of faith and trust were birthed. May this book be a symbol of manifested dreams and God given gifts for all who read this and may these poetic verses be an inspiration to you.

CONTENTS

ACKNOWLEDGMENTS

I want to acknowledge my mother who has supported my dreams, my brother who listens to my dreams, and my daughter who is the propelling force that motivates me to put in the work to make them come true.

"Writers aren't exactly people… They're a whole bunch of people trying to be one person."

F. Scott Fitzgerald

REFLECTIONS

As one works creatively, the creative process itself may not undergo much change, however, the creation itself can change and often it does change. It changes in the hands of the creator as it is formed and it changes in the hands and minds of those who partake in it based on how they perceive it. In essence, as we all grow and thereby obtain a wealth of experiences, subsequently our perspectives change. Therefore, what motivates us changes over time based on our stations in life and thus those things that inspire us are constantly changing as well.

I have good reason for my introductory disclaimer on creative change mainly as it relates to this book of poetry and also as it relates to the arts as a whole and to life. Essentially this book offers a look into my perception of life and my growth through poetry as a literary creative medium. As I began writing and putting together this book of poetry and pondering what title would be most appropriate, I first considered writing a reflection to accompany each piece in order to give the reader my interpretation and clear reasoning behind each one. However, I changed my mind. I decided against doing so for what I felt was a very important reason as it relates to poetry as a literary art form. Art evokes emotion. Literary art evokes emotion through words. Words paint pictures in our minds. These painted mental pictures are different for each of us depending on how we interpret what we read. Our interpretations depend on our perspectives which are based on our own personal experiences.

Simply put, I did not want to rob the reader of the opportunity to make their own interpretations. To do so would be to rob them of the intimate experience with the poems. Although I do in fact have my own reasoning behind why I chose to write the poems and I know what I was feeling at the time that I wrote them, I decided that I wanted to give the reader the opportunity to develop their own feelings. I did not want the reader to simply read what I as the writer intended for each piece to mean, but for the reader to discover what each piece means to them.

Still, some thoughts that I would like to offer about this book of poetry is that each poem has come from a place within me that reflects my own personal experiences on my journey towards purpose, consciousness, self-love, and self-awareness. The words illustrate through their description my growth through life as well as the insight and perceptions that I have gained along my journey thus far.

Indeed, I am still a wayfarer on this road of life as we all are. I am still growing and learning new things about the world and about myself with each new experience. These poems are in no way definitive in thought. Indeed until we leave this earth we are always learning and growing and hopefully opening up to new ideas through our experiences which change our perceptions and inspire us in a positive way. I would like to think however, that I have come to a place in my life where I am much more wise and discerning as a result of the situations that I have overcome, that I am much more knowledgeable of who I am and what I want out of life, and that I have reached a level in my faith where I know without a shadow of a doubt that with God anything is possible and that everything will be alright no matter how bad things seem to be in our present moments.

To that point, many times human beings can share very similar experiences with one another and yet still interpret them in very different ways. Although my personal experiences in life are not unlike many of the experiences that others have faced, these poems are my own reflection of those experiences. Each one reflects my experiences in life with love and desire, being a woman, a mother, being a believer in Jesus, my belief in God, my dreams, my joys, my fears, and my overall existence as a human being. As a result, because my life is extremely multifaceted, at times what comes out in my writing may seem controversial and contradictory, yet it is indicative of every area of my life and my perspective of my experience. It's not that I am inconsistent or that any of us as human beings are purposely inconsistent, it simply means that each relationship is different, each situation is different, and that as time passes so do our stations in life.

At times I've been in love, at other times I've had my heart broken and yet during those times I am still a nurturing mother, I am a needy daughter, I am a supportive friend who likes to have wild fun, I am a dreamer, I am a strong but very passionate woman, I am a woman of color, I am an advocate, a fighter, and through it all I am still a devoted child of God. My poetry reflects every bit of that. It makes up every part of me. It reflects what makes me happy. It reflects my hopes and dreams, my struggles, my fears, my failures, and my imperfections. It reflects me. It reflects my life. How might it reflect yours? If you will, I invite you to share in my insights and delight in my words. Join me on this road to becoming me…

MY LIFE

As I look upon it
My mind's eye doth see
A wide road paved before me
An endless sky with limitless possibility
Strength and knowledge to overtake thee
As long as God so guides me
My life
I will live
Fully, purposefully, and...
Completely

JUST LET ME

I can't see where the sky begins or where it ends
My boundaries are out of focus
I'm nearsighted and farsighted all at the same time
I could fly or free fall
All
At the same time
Free me
Don't catch me
Don't save me
Don't stop me
Just let me
fly
Just let me
fall
Just let me
Discover all
That God has intended me to be...

HER IN THE MIRROR

What you see is what she has spoken
The person you encounter is who she has believed she is
She is an exact replica of everything she thinks
Her body is a physical representation
A physical manifestation of that which is unseen on the inside of her
She cannot deny it
And neither can you
The girl in the mirror
That girl is you
Learn her
Love her
Sanctify her

RECKLESS LIFE

We ought not to live life with such reckless abandon
Foregoing our power and rights
In constant zeal let me consciously live
By love, knowledge, and might
Let my life reveal
An adventurous tale
Of glorious victorious wars
And when I am old
Let my story be told
I lived purposely, bold, and free

THE APOLOGY

Standing on your backs and shoulders
I bemoan what my life has become
Out of the unfortunate circumstances brought on
By my own failure to see, that what is inside of me…
Is an ultimate, never ending, unfailing, phenomenally,
Ever present, diehard spirit of a female warrior meant to be
Royal
Created by God after an image of Godliness next to man whose help
Is found in
No one
But me…

How can I apologize for the unfathomable disregard
Of the regality flowing through my veins?
That which before me was shed
Both by Christ
And my ancestors,
My forefathers,
And my foremothers…
It is not my spiritual eyes with which I see
But my physical ones which cause me to misperceive
That which had long ago been made clear by the history
Written on the pages, told in the stories, and the scars on the backs
Of those who came before me…

How can I correct my own misguidance?
How can I begin again to honor myself and your legacy?
How do I begin again to honor my lineage and continue to bring forth
leaders
Instead of children who suffer
Mentally and emotionally at the hand of my own disrespect of myself?
Ignorant of who I am thus they being ignorant of who they are
And how do I begin again to honor my destiny, so that God may join
me with Kings
That will bring me into their own royal courts
Instead of connecting with lost souls who lack the willingness,
knowledge, revelation, and
ability

to be leaders in their own right?

How do I...?

And yet,
Despite your legacy,
It is with my own strength that I must stand up
And live
Consciously.
Consciously aware of what I am made of, what I have come from…
So that from this descent
I may arrive at my destined place
And after this life
In that eternal place
I can look into your face
And rejoice
I was the promise
And
I made it

A NEW FIGHT

Acts of solidarity keep us satisfied
We play new games with old rules
Never quite realizing the intelligent mix
Between
X and King
Peace yet action
Faith yet work
Always be in action
And fight when you must
Clubs, hoses, dogs and nooses are so old school
Now systemic barriers are the new age conquering tools
March on Washington, march on Jena, march on Sanford, march on
who?
March for who? March for what?
Do we really have a clue?
And are we really serious?
Or are we just content
Are we only seeking to keep the movement relevant?
Or were we truly meant
To change the events
That threaten to repeat history?
New games, new rules, new fight
Fulfilling the purpose of our own destiny
Carrying the torch for our equality
Against systemic weapons of mass destruction
Meet
The leaders of the NEW school
New Day
New Age
New Fight

THE PRESSING

She is at the threshing floor
Her feet are tired and bare
Her hair hangs low
Arching her back
She yields to the sky
God, I beg of you no more!
A beating from the heat of the sun
Whipped by the winds of change
Downcast by grey skies
Drenched by the rain
Held down by circumstance
Withheld from a chance
In agony she endures it all
She is at the threshing floor
Her time has come for the pressing
The pressing
The pressing
The pressing
God has summoned her for a pressing
A pressing
A pressing
A pressing
And when she has given it up
And when He has taken it all
The fruit of what will remain
Is the fruit from a harvest of gold

THE ANTIDOTE

It came in the tiniest of bottles
It was small yet mighty indeed
Tied down
Still…
I winced, screamed, and struggled
Words of comfort I would not believe
Unaware of a way to deny it
Of this in my heart I was sure
I knew I would have to endure it
For my health would depend on its cure
I knew I would have to receive it
Or the healing could never take place
The needle pierced my skin like a razor
Like fire it seeped through my veins
I screamed for my life
"Please don't do this!"
But its work had already begun
It seemed worse than the lies that had ailed me
For so long the lies had me numb
I was numbed to the realities of truth
And this antidote is truth undenied
For without it, man cannot be helped
To refuse is restoration declined

THE OLD MAN

The old man before me
Is pushed towards the light
Overtaken
Dead on impact
He gave up the fight
Limp at my feet
Crying and wailing
And yet I knew
He was stagnant and stubborn
The old man had to die

He had ceased in growing
His bowels were locked up tight
He rejected the promise
And held on to past rights
He was content in the moment
Celebrating days long gone by
It became quite clear
The old man had to die

His fate was sealed
He would come this way no more
The old man would not grow accustomed
To all this life had in store
He would reject its promise
And utter his disbeliefs
He would fear the victory
Of his own blessed seed
He would even appeal the benefits of long awaited progress

Indeed, the old man was…
Incessantly bitter and hopeless
Yet try as he might
To recapture the past life
It was without question
The old man had to die

THE SEARCH

Searching myself through my failures
Through each stumble, each trip, and each fall
And maybe…
Just maybe…
I'll find it
An answer that confirms it all
I'm trying to locate my purpose
My reason for being at all
Yet my efforts…
They only confound me
As I diligently search through this life
Not knowing just what I'll discover
Grasping hold to the glimmers of light
On this path
I glean clues and learn lessons
Shaping my constant metamorphosis of being
And with diligence my search will continue
Through life's plains, its mountains, and valleys
And my souvenirs of hope and experience
Will forever my fervor maintain
And each day I'll continue my quest
To realize that which is within
An ultimate treasure of purpose
The essence and call of all men

GUNNING FOR THE GAUNTLET

I have resolved that it seems
My dreams
Are directing me towards certain demise
How can I run towards the height of life?
Naive and ill prepared for the uncertainties that await me
I am gunning for the gauntlet
God give me the courage
God give me the strength
God give me the instinct
God give me the knowledge
God give me the will
I am gunning for the gauntlet
I am aiming towards a flogging
Of criticism
Of doubt
Of disbelief
Of disapproval
And reproach
I am gunning for the gauntlet
I am gunning for my dreams

BACK TO THE DRAWING BOARD

Dismantle the incomplete frame
Unhinge the unyielding door
We've nothing to lose for the growing
It's back to the drawing board

Don't fret the rebuilding in life
A set back is much more than this
A chance to enhance the foundation
Opportunity that should not be missed

Together let's forge a new destiny
Together let's strengthen the fight
We'll sing of how we got over
Through trials, and failures, and strife

Each day is a chance for renewal
Reshaping and creating success
We've nothing to gain from surrender
We've nothing to be but the best

And again we will see things much clearer
Than ever we saw them before
Through our tests we've garnered much wisdom
It's back to the drawing board

RENAISSANCE CHILD

I AM
the daughter of Jessie Fauset
and Zora Neale
You see...
I came from many mothers
Many mothers
Many, many, MANY mothers
And like an overdue babe
I burst through their wombs like plastic stretched too thin
on water balloons
And I soon
came forth
with my pen and my paper
And my thoughts
The rebirth of a Renaissance
Like my father Langston Hughes
I soothe
The soul
My father he is
He was
And
I AM
The promised child
of Countee, of Georgia,
of Dubois, and Jessie
Arna, and Alice
Of Anne and James
My verses flowing free like the river Zambezi
Wild and untamed
Yet contained within the sacred reservoir of a legacy known as
The greatest of all time
They are
And
I AM
The Renaissance Child

MULTIDIMENSIONAL

I am so many different things.
I am so many different people.
I have so many titles.
Daughter
Mother
Sister
Friend
Teacher
Partner
Counselor
Woman
I am made in God's image.
Like the trinity,
I am many parts
And yet
I am one
I am the only me there will ever be
And yet
I am
Multidimensional

HER LIGHT

A light she keeps
Though soft and dim
In her lamp throughout the night
She is always hopeful
Yet never too eager, to make her presence known
She is solemn yet dreams of a happier place where love is free in being
She is cautious yet fearless to take on the darkness though demons lurk
unseen
Yet what is this power in her soft illumination that calmly demands to
be noticed?
Her spirit?
Her soul?
Her God from within?
What secrets does she hold?
And what of her love that she longs to give?
Can its fullness and depth be compared?
It seems not to any on this side of heaven
Tis epically unparalleled

THE MISSISSIPPI IN ME

The Mississippi in me lies deep within
It stained me
Yet birthed me and raised me
It's a part of me deeply
And that I cannot deny
Even if I should try
I could never let it go
It's part of who I am
And I am partially unhinged
Feeling conflicted
From the stench of its wretched past
Never forgotten
Never forgiven
Volatile
Yet comforting
Like the balmy wind before a thunderstorm
I am torn
She is my mother yet she is my enemy
And when I leave, I miss her
And when I come to her, I love her
And when they speak of her, I resent her
And still…
It birthed me and raised me
It's a part of me deeply
I cannot deny
And even if I should try
I could never let it go
It's part of who I am
Very simply
It lies within me
Mississippi

FAMILIAR FIGHT

The struggle latched on
It would not let her go
Fighting an old familiar demon
The root of the word wouldn't seem to grow
It reinforced her trouble
With insecurity
Thinking this was the finale
Of all that she could be
The hope of a dream too big
She dared not believe
Fighting an old familiar demon
Uprooting the curse of a bad seed
And forever it would seem
She'd fight this battle tooth and nail
She did everything natural
To ensure she would prevail
Still with loud resistance
The voice in her head did yell
Fighting an old familiar demon
Bearing her cross, she must not fail

MY EXAMPLE

All of my mistakes made transparent
All of my sins laid bare
My experiences are an open book
To know, to learn, to share
I am a road map
An example
Of what God can do
Impressing upon me
Imprinting upon you
And with this life, I'll indelibly shine
Illuminating and celebrating this life of mine
An act of worship to the Divine
My words and my work
Through the use of my power
To lead, teach, and inspire
For this is my God given deed
Every day to live, to fight
To affect and to believe
To pattern my example
By honoring that which is within me

THE HARDEST THING

The courage to be me
The courage to stand tall
The courage to fight
The courage to believe
The courage to continue
The courage to share
The courage to trust
And the courage to love
No matter the task
No matter the test
No matter the trial
Or what may come on tomorrow
The hardest thing
The most difficult thing
Is having the courage to be me as I brave it all

FROM THE DUST

Seeds of greatness emerge
Fertile and fruitful
Yielding to the elements of sunshine and rain
Grow
Stand tall
Burgeon and bloom
Let not your seed be disregarded
Nor crushed underfoot
Let man experience your glory
See your beauty
Smell your fragrance
Let not the sower grieve His efforts to nurture your existence
You were planted with purpose
Let it nurture and empower
Cultivating only positive for gain
And from the dust you shall rise
A garden of beauty
A harvest of delight
A flourishing bouquet
Coming forth with stems of honor
Adorned with petals of wisdom
Clad and arrayed in colorful might

SING AND SHOUT

Sing and Shout
Of this beautiful existence
Of this beautiful experience
Of this beautiful coincidence
Of this beautiful chance
Sing and shout
I love,
I love.
I love!
Everything!!
Humble and naïve
Blissfully ignorant
Simple and serene
Eager and stout
Taste and see
Laugh and dance
Breathe in, breathe out
Sing and shout
Tis what life is all about.

THE BLESSING OF MINE

My child pay attention
It is easy to miss
As you journey through life
Take heed to this
In the chaos of the day
In the closeness of danger
In the odd coincidence
Of a familiar stranger
It is there you'll find
The blessing of Mine

It is My protection and preservation
As you go about your day
When evil seeks to devour you
As you pass along its way
It is endowment and favor
That I give only to you
When what you truly deserved
Had finally come due
It is there you'll find
The blessing of Mine

It is my exception and pardon
When you've knowingly done wrong
When the laws of My universe
Are stern and strong
It is the knowledge and wisdom
And a word of confirmation
When circumstances seem to drown you
In overwhelming confusion
It's the quiet peace
In the middle of the night
When stress rests on your chest
And you're tired of the fight
It's a word of encouragement
From that special someone
When you've failed after trying

With all your might

So my child…
Pay attention
It is easy to miss
As you journey through life
Take heed to this
Listen to my voice
Deep down inside
It is there you'll find
The blessing of Mine

ELUSIVE

She fades in and out of memory
Like smoke wafting through the air
She burns from the fire within
Longing to be noticed
Yet moves in and out of sight
Her power is in her mystery
Vague and indescribable
She produces wonder with the magic of her words
Her mind is a jewel that intrigues even the wisest of men
She evades all limits and bounds
She dares not be contained
Yet still
She longs to be noticed
By the one who would seek to find her
Hoping that the fire within her
Will burn bright enough
For the one who longs for her warmth and dares for her challenge
Elusive

WHEN OUR WORLDS COLLIDE

When East meets West
Our worlds collide
Our hemispheres draw near
Our realms are made manifest
As we delight in intimate discoveries

We explore the terrain of
Boundless love
Its mountains and valleys
Its beautiful plains

Our love is solid
Like terra firma
So much to discover
It is terra incognita
With multiple treasures

We welcome love's invasion
Its extraterrestrial experience
The universe expands
The Pleiades are shaken

Crashing into each other
Our lives forever changed
Life's landscape altered
When our worlds collide

HEART ON MY SLEEVE

A fervent desire for life
Has me busting at the seams
I snatch my own heart out of my own chest
And I wear it on my sleeve
My arms, hands, and fingers are red with my own blood
Grabbing hold of all that is dear to me
Staining it red with my intensity
Some admire my self-sacrifice
Others look at me in horror
And some don't miss the opportunity
To take advantage of my vulnerability
I could place my heart back in its rightful place
And close up the gaping hole
I could wash away the blood and appear sane and whole
But on the outside it beats brave and bold
It cusps greatness in its ventricles
Craving the surreal
Dying for the thrill
Heart on my sleeve
Feel it beating in my embrace

SHINE

So let the light shine
Let it shine upon my face
Let this conscious existence
Be my full embrace
Of God's gift of life
Of His offer of love
Let me taste sweet freedom
Granted from heaven above

OCEAN OF LOVE

Wading in a sea of vulnerability
Love envelopes me
And I drown in it
Face down
Head first
And although it may break me
And be the death of me
I freely give to it my trust
And something happens
Receiving me
The strength of love in turn
Supports me
Stronger than I imagined
And love,
Creating buoyancy
Causes me to float...
Endlessly
Again
To the top
And through the up and down waves of love
I float endlessly
Giving it my all
Surrendering to its current
I am overtaken in its deep expanse
Overtaken in an ocean of love
Over
And over
And over
Again

ALMOND BUTTER BROWN

Almond butter brown baby of mine
God has given to me
A blessing divine

Almond butter brown girl
Baby so sweet
Raising you in this world
Will be no small feat

Almond butter brown child
So beautiful and bold
Never be discouraged
Embrace your dreams and break the mold

Almond butter brown love
Maintain your innocence and peace
It will be a buffer to this world
Through trouble, dismay, and grief

Almond butter brown angel
My pride and my joy
Delighting in your birth
Motivating me all the more

Almond butter brown heart
My heiress of tomorrow
May your light shine bright
May your blessings trump your sorrows

Almond Butter Brown
My Ava
Dream big
Take the limits off of God
Realize more than mommy ever did

MARTYRED MOTHER'S SECRETS

In between the legs of pious mothers lies
Fire for life and love
And indiscretions in disguise
Covered by silk stockings
Time and bitterness had been her demise
But drama and desire behind tired eyes
Gave clues to a life fully lived in the heat under southern skies
Her pursed lips were tormented with the secrets of her martyred
existence
Settling for an upright living
Submitting herself to stringent religion
She often resented the smiles of bold and silly young women
Though foolish and unwise, they had the courage she didn't
If only she could go back
Perhaps make some different decisions
These secrets wouldn't hold her down
Unable to be swayed from her mission
Her purpose
Her gifts
The desires of her heart
A life more clearly defined by God's vision
Powerful
Passionate
A reason for living
This she had longed for
And now she lamented
In the quiet of the night
Held tight within her bosom
Martyred Mother's Secrets

SATURATED

I see you in my dreams
And smell the scent of your skin in a passing breeze…
I taste your lips as I touch myself
And I feel your hands
And their security
The strength in your arms
The calming gaze that radiates from your eyes
I am saturated with love for you
Overwhelmed by my need for you
My heart is overflowing
It spills and stains
Our hearts, our hands, our faces, our bodies
Drenching our senses
I need you like air
I desire you like a sweet nectar
You arouse the secrets within me
I am not my own

THIS ALCATRAZ

Loneliness like an island
A tortured feeling of angst
Hanging on to your every word
Watching your every move
I constantly seek perfection for you
Not from within
But without
Not for the good of me
But for the satisfaction of you
Wasted time and too many compromises
Shutting out wisdom and self-love
But this was love
Or so I thought
No one could tell me any different
Ruled by emotion
Too blind to realize
That the pieces don't fit
Abuse me
Betray me
Misuse me
Love me so bad
Until I long for freedom
And I hasten to let this go
Until my dreams turn into nightmares
And I want no more
Until the fire inside me has fizzled and dimmed
And I break out of this prison
This Alcatraz

MISTAKEN SOUL

Soul Mistaken
Do souls make mistakes?
I don't know
It feels like I've been mistaken
Too many times before
Over and over
My soul declares
My heart rejoices
In the knowledge it shares
Succumbing to faulty discernment
Shattered by tawdry affairs
Do souls make mistakes?
I don't know
But mine must have
Yes…
It must have been mistaken
Mistaken soul
Soul mate
Mistaken

A WISH

I had a vision of you
But...
It quickly slipped away
What is ever more fleeting than a fantasy and a daydream?
A heartbeat perhaps?
Oh how I wish it would remain

I wish that my illusions would somehow materialize
I wish I wasn't so heartbroken
I wish the good wasn't so hard to realize
Oh how can this dream remain?

I think of us in those dark moments
When everything seems so lost
It gives me hope in the myth of love
Whilst I bear my cross

But the truth I know
Of naïve ideas
As I face reality's glare
Is that nothing's more fleeting than a fantasy and a daydream
Oh...
How I wish it would remain
You and I

THE FROST

Ice on the windows of my soul
I cannot see clearly through the cold
Arctic chills emitting from my chest
My heart is frozen
No one can break though
Not even me
I've tried time and time again
Wading through the tears
Trudging through the pain
Tip toeing through blood stained shards of a cracked heart and a broken
soul
Picking up the pieces
Resisting the truth
Of what it will take just to put it all back together again
And what I must face so that the light will shine in
Still…
No one dares tread on the pathway towards this heart
It is a desolate place
The frost has taken hold
Frozen

AND I DIDN'T REMEMBER

And I didn't remember your name
And I didn't remember the pain
Labor without gain
Forgiveness was my delivery
And joy I held in my arms
Kisses of gratefulness poured from my lips
And love I kept in my heart
And peace was stayed on my mind
And I didn't remember the trouble
And I didn't remember his name

PRETTY UNINTENDED

Crafted beauty deep within
Welling up to reach the surface
She appears in her lifetime
A mother, a queen
Though virtually unseen
Shrouded in the poise of honor and dignity
Wearing accessories of strength and resilience
Weakness a strange bedfellow
Failure and death were never her options
Her neck, long and graceful to swallow the pride
Her hips round and wide to carry the load of an unborn nation
Her stomach soft and round to cushion weary kings
Her breasts large with milk to sustain the warriors of the people
She was called many things but pretty
Pretty was unintended
Her voice was deep
From her lips flowed words of wisdom
Her eyes saw all that was deep beneath the surface
She was more than a helpmate
She was a necessary queen consort
Pretty was unintended
Pretty was never the purpose
She is more than a vain exhibition
She is queen and fellow warrior
Her beauty was natural
Pretty
Was
Unintended
Pretty
Was
Never
The
Purpose
Love and power were her purpose
Beauty was a bonus
Pretty unintended

PASSION AND PAIN

It is this that has soothed me
Tortures and afflicts me
They are one in the same
My passion and pain
It has freed me and chained me
It completes and consoles me
Yet it unravels me at the grain
My passion and pain
From my heart it has taken
The essence of me
What have I to gain?
My passion and pain
I pray that it remains
An outlet of dear expression
A gift that is worth
Priceless impressions
Let it not be in vain
My passion and pain

REBEL STAR

Don't box me in
I'll break out
And smash your box to smithereens
I'm a rebel
Like King David
Warring against the Philistines
Who could even know me well enough?
I can barely constrain myself
My knowledge is ever growing
My passion is overflowing
Creative freedom is essential to my health
The universe is my sandbox
The atmosphere is my gate
We're created by the same being
I cannot be contained
And your ignorance I cannot indemnify
It remains so puzzling to me
Of one's need to comfort their inhibitions
By rejecting any possibility
Of our God granted abilities
And the powers that we hold
Behold
That which is within you
Freedom and light
I am and you are
A
Rebel Star

PAGES AND ROADS

Endless pages, empty spaces
Blank sheets and open lines
Fresh emotions and new ideas
Notations of love and life
Expressions of hopes and dreams
Accounts of experience
Descriptions of sadness and joy
Portraits of thoughts and feelings
Through words
Words of life
Words like maps
Maps of roads and journeys
Through heartaches and celebrations
Expectations and failures
Maps
Maps of words
Words of life

BY THE TIME YOU READ THIS

By the time you read this
I will have found myself
Yet still evolving
I surround myself
With truth, light, and love
And with these gifts
I maintain myself
Through the trials
And I remind myself
That I have been groomed for this moment
This purpose
A daughter, an heiress
To the throne of grace
If you are reading this
I have found myself
Through the light and love
Of God's embrace

www.ingramcontent.com/pod-product-compliance
Lightning Source LLC
Chambersburg PA
CBHW021226020426
42331CB00003B/486